CATHOLIC RELIGION

- after 2nd Vatican Council

Jakob Munck

CATHOLIC RELIGION

- after 2nd Vatican Council

2015

© 2015 Jakob Munck - www.jamu.dk
Vers: 150530
Forlag: Books on Demand GmbH, København, Danmark
Tryk: Books on Demand GmbH, Norderstedt, Tyskland
ISBN: 9788771702347

Indhold

1. INTRODUCTION

Dear Reader.

To me to be Catholic is to believe that man is good, that we have free will, that we are all loved by God and that all people - regardless of religion - can be saved. Churches are cultural institutions which have a therapeutic and a social task to solve. It is a community and its liturgy, sacraments and all its theology is arranged such that it caters to people who feel they are "sinners" and who wants to be cleansed of the burden that they thereby have put on themselves.

A good Catholic is a Catholic who thinks for himself, who is critical and has not made the Catholic religion into his livelihood and thus has put themselves in a financially beholden to the local bishop. Such people are - unfortunately - very hard to find.

The opposite of a good Catholic is a papist. Papists are people who cultivate a unique religion. In the old days they called such people "ultra montanists" ("over the mountains"), because they sought to propagate the view that the Pope is infallible (like Muhammad) and that critical thinking therefore is dangerous. Critical thinking leads - after the Papists' opinion - to schismatic perceptions, and because salvation is only possible if one is in full communion with the Roman Church, then it is wise to put his own sense on standby to avoid ending up in hell.

But the Popish doctrine is false. It is irreconcilable with the Christian faith and because I confess myself to this faith, it is a pleasure to me to give a modest contribution to its development, trying to follow the ideals of Jesus Christ and His Holy Mother Mary.

Jakob Munck

2. ONE POPE TWO CHURCHES

When in 1995 I went to be taught by Catholic nun about catholic faith, I asked several times for a text, which could briefly inform me what Catholics believe in. But it was not so easy to satisfy my need. Certainly they had documents from the last church-council, but they filled approximately 500 pages and covered a range of things that no longer was quite timely, since Vatican II had ended 30 years ago. I could also read the church's catechism, which had just been published in Norwegian, but it consisted of 2,600 clauses, and was a little too bulky. Of course there was the Bible, but my teacher made it clear to me that Catholics do not uncritical "believe in the Bible" just as some Protestants do. For Catholics, it is the tradition and teaching of the Church, which is in the center, the Bible is more some kind of historical source for the doctrine. Therefore, there is much in the Bible that Catholics do not believe in, at least not if it is to be taken literally. Paul believed, for example that women should not speak in public, and several of the prophets in the Old Testament recommend murder and war on the holy people's opponents. But the church does not believe in that.

But what does one believe in? I was told that I could read the Creed, then I would get a good impression of what Catholics believe, and this advice I followed. Here they had a brief formulation of the Church's teaching, and although many of the sentences in this declaration sounded strange and was not quite easy to understand, then this was a starting point. So the question was thus about whether this statement should be interpreted symbolically, metaphorically or literally, and I could not get a clear answer to this, so I came to terms with that the viewpoint that one has to decide for himself. If you could say the Creed, without feeling that you were lying, then you are a Catholic and a supporter of the Catholic faith, I was told.

In the coming years, I found out that the question of what Catholics believe was not only hard for my teacher to answer, but that this issue was one of the main themes of all Catholic debates. There were many different viewpoints, and ultimately every Catholic has his own view. I became informed that this and that perception was not consistent with "church teaching." On the whole, the concept of "church teaching" took a big part of the dispute. Some believed it and others did not. But it might not matter as long as the different directions still - after all - was so close to each other that they could participate in the same Mass. Because it is the Mass and the service which is at the heart of the Catholic Church, and those who cannot or will not participate in this ceremony, cannot fully count themselves as Catholics. What Catholics believe, my teacher taught me, that is what is said during Mass and all the rest are considered to be private views which you can decide whether to believe or not.

I gradually found out that there was a certain pattern and that Catholics can broadly be divided into two segments, which formally belong to the same church, but which in practice are very different. These two directions believe different things about the Christian morality, the Mass' liturgy, other religions, morals, the Pope, the Jews and the church's role in the modern world. Being an active Catholic is to participate in an ever-running debate on these and other topics that relate to the question that I started to ask my teacher: What does Catholics believe in? It was not only me who had doubts about this, so had she, and also the church in general.

As the years passed my experience showed me that the Catholic faith and its followers can be divided into two main streams which are opposed to each other, and therefore expect each other to be heretical, old-fashioned and immoral, each of which wants to conquer the church and - if possible - to shut the others out. In the beginning of my Catholic career, I was mostly under the influence of one direction, the liberals, while I in course of time became increasingly oriented towards the traditionalist. Personally, I experienced this as a learning process, and today I perceive the liberal Catholics as being naive, un-Christian and Judaic. On the other hand, I am also sure that many of them perceive me as being conservative and Anti-Semitic. I think they are wrong just like they probably think that I am wrong.

In the following we will not deal with my personal experiences. I will try to describe the two mutually contradictory interpretations of the Catholic faith that I have met in the church. That the followers of these directions mutually despise each other and tries to shut each other out, is due to their different understandings of a number of crucial questions of moral, theological and historical nature, and these are the issues that we will deal with.

Maybe I'm not a completely neutral observer, but on the other hand, it is not my job to judge which of the two described directions that is the correct one. I try to describe them as good as I can, and so the reader can form his own opinion. I can say that I do not uniquely belong to either one or the other of these directions.

What is always true in conflicts is the question of what the one and the other side of the dispute shall be referred to as, is a subject of disagreement. You could call the two trends for liberals and traditionalists. But you can also designate them as being humanists and fundamentalists, left- and right-wing anarchists and moralists or Philo-Semites and Anti-Semites. Each of these conceptual pairs says something true about the contrast that exists between the factions, but one should be aware that the contradictions between the supporters of the two wings are not so great that they do not fall within the same church. They all have the same pope, but there are significant differences in how they interpret their relationship with this man in the Vatican.

The choice of name for the two wings and the way we characterize them, says something about where you are standing, because words are not neutral. None of the above names are adequate for the full contents of the two faiths, but all say something true. Actually, I should choose to designate them with numbers 1 and 2, as it would sound neutral, but it would also seem a bit artificial. Therefore, I instead choose to use the terms "liberals" and "traditionalists". What you will choose to call the two directions, you must decide after you has formed an impression. The fact is that what is important is the content. It's about what the Catholic faith is about, and what it should comprise. The question is whether there today is a single Catholic church, or whether it is more correct to talk about two? The latter I believe in and I hope so, because I would not like to have to subordinate me a majority that I do not like. I acknowledge that there is only one pope in Rome, but I do not recognize that this pope - or other ecclesiastical authorities - always tells the truth. History and my own experience have taught me that it is not the case. Schism is therefore not only a bad thing, because it leads to discussion and clarification. If the church should shift and not just petrify in a past form, it is necessary to open up the debate which the present text suggests. But many would prefer to protect their power and the notion that the ecclesiastical authority is infallible. It claims to be, when ruling on metaphysical dogmas, but beyond that, so it is just as fallible as any other authority. But, it is unfortunately not all Catholics who have the courage to face this.

And hereby we go to the description of Catholicism two main directions, which they appear at the beginning of the third millennium. What one can argue about is the following:

* The Mass and its purpose

Liberals believe that the purpose of the Catholic Church's service - first and foremost - is the social community between church members. The divine service must therefore take place in a liturgical form that is a reminiscent of a circle, where the priest and the Mass' other participants see each other and communicate with each other. However, it is not only to meet each other, people go to the Mass, because God's Word and Sacrament have a meaning. The priest's sermon is a kind of moral rearmament, and it is therefore essential that he have the word of his power. And the sacrament acts like a kind of fixed point, which the faithful gather around to hear the sermon and to meet each other.

The belief in God's presence in the sacrament - according to the liberal's perception - is a way to create emotional liberation of the believers and to provide them with psychological benefits of the aisle. The liberalists are of course like any other, followers of the doctrine about the bread transformation into the Body of Christ (transubstantiation), but do not expect this teaching of particular importance. They believe that it is an expression of empty scholastic, if one distinguishes between the Lutheran and Catholic Sacrament' doctrine, and they therefore also believe that all Christians - whether they are Catholic or not - must have access to participate in the sacrament.

Traditionalists believe that the purpose of the Mass is to worship God, and not significantly to meet or communicate with each other. It transformed remedy - the body of Christ - can be taken equally well in and outside the church, because the sacrament has a healing effect on those who receives it. Participants in the Mass turns his face in the same direction, namely towards the Blessed Sacrament and the modern liturgical handshake (greeting of peace) is not used. On the other hand it is argued that the sacrament has a saving effect of the believers, recalling the impact that drugs have on sick people. Why it works so well, no one knows, because it is a mystery. But without a regular intake of the consecrated Host, one cannot live. Traditionalists stresses on the importance of bread transformation and the sacred content in the sacrament. It is believed that the Lutheran doctrine that rejects transubstantiation is heretical and that non-Catholics should not have access to receive the Body of Christ.

* Ecumenism

Liberals believe that anyone can go to heaven, and that there therefore is no particular reason to be baptized or to convert to the Catholic faith. Baptism is not a necessary condition for salvation, and it is not possible to designate one religion as being more authentic or nearer God than the other. This theology separates itself heavily from Islam, which they believe is violent and womandiscriminatory, and claims that this religion is a common enemy of Christians and Jews. One prefers religion, which does not have an authoritarian leadership or too strictly defined dogmas. Therefore one usually means that Protestantism is an equally good form of Christianity as Catholicism. Lutherans are not heretics, but only Christians of a different shade than the Catholics. Therefore, the conversion from the Protestant sects and to the Catholic Church makes no greater sense since one is as good as another.

Traditionalists believe that the salvation's option exclusively, or primarily, is located in the Catholic Church. It is believed that Jesus is right, when he demands baptism and the intake of the sacrament as a prerequisite for people to go to heaven. Traditionalists see no important purpose of ecumenical work, as this often leads to the false impression among participants that one religion is as good as the others. And they mean that this is not true. It certainly cannot be the Catholics' assignment to make advertising of non-Christian faiths and if you have to attend some forms of ecumenical activity, it must therefore be solely for the purpose of converting the other participants who have not yet seen the truth in Jesus Christ and the Catholic Church.

* Virgin Mary

Liberalists have an unresolved relationship with the Virgin Mary, which they don't like to call "Mother of God". Partly, there is a tendency to Arianism amongst liberals, that is, the belief that Jesus was only human, and partly one estimates the theological teachings of resurrection and sinless birth to be a kind of myth or superstition, rather than historical reality. Moreover, it is not uncommon for the liberals, to estimate the whole Catholic faith to be a kind of sacred poetry and thus the doctrine of Jesus as God's son and the resurrection and ascension, to be a pious tale without basis in historical reality. Therefore, one is not enthusiastic about the doctrine of the Virgin Mary as Mother of God, as it suggests that Jesus was not just a human being. In the liberal churches one will often see that statues of Mary either completely absent or that they are replaced by modernist paintings or renaissance reliefs with unclear relation to the Holy Mother, which can thus leave it to the believer's own imagination to place a depiction on. As a rule the priest dislikes that believers spend too much time on the Blessed Virgin, because everything this saint does is to refer to her son, they say, and so you may as well ask him directly. Herein, they agree with the Protestants.

Traditionalists love Mary, which they like to refer to as Mother of God. They consider her to be the church's common mother and teacher and theology is just a kind of substitute for the true Mariological faith. There are traditionalists who love Mary so deeply that they see her as being associated with the Trinity itself, but usually she is only perceived as an expression of the loving, maternal, and thus for the best of the woman in the family, and - in a wider perspective - in the church. As one does not believe that the study of theology in itself is a beneficial service, they often only lead the faithful to prayer and nothing is more relevant than the praying to the Virgin Mary. In churches with traditionalist settings, there will always be a beautiful and realistic Mary-figure, and preferably icons with artistic views of the beautiful Mother of God, which the faithful loves to kneel and pray to.

* Lutheranism

Liberals believe that Lutheranism is an unfortunate departure from the Catholic faith, but that this doctrine is basically true. One does not believe that there are fundamental contradictions between the Catholic and Lutheran faith, and not infrequently is it argued that it was mainly the Roman Pope's error, which was a result of that the Reformation took place. Lutheranism is not interested in succession they have women priests and do not believe that human's sin is of such a nature that it can be removed through confession. They also rejects penance, indulgences and religious pilgrimages and believes that man only to a limited extent has free will. All this, perhaps excluding the doctrine of the "enslaved will", the liberals agree on. Traditionalists believe that there are critical differences between Catholic and Lutheran faith, and that the two faiths differ so much apart that it is required up to a year of teaching and Catholic practice for the repentant Protestants, that he can be admitted to the Catholic Church. Traditionalists prefer to call people who are transferred from Lutheran churches to Catholic for "converts", although this word has disappeared from the church's official language. Today the church usually recognizes baptism in the Lutheran congregations (at least in Denmark), and thus does not require rebaptism of being admitted. But many traditionalists would argue that this still would be a good idea. For the sacraments have an almost magical effect, and living with a non-valid baptism is a serious thing. In the end, it can prevent the believer's access to heaven.

* Moral

Liberals believe that the church is first and foremost an expression of a cultural tradition and that it will serve as a social gathering point for its members. It is recognized that the church has moral standards, but they do not believe that these standards have a binding character. Most liberals therefore believe that divorce and re-marrying is allowed and many also believe that the church should not deal with abortion, since this area must be the woman's private choice.

The decisive bid in the liberal morality is this love, which says that one should love one's neighbor as oneself. But what this love in practice consists of is there disagreement about. They usually allege that they support equality and tolerance and the human right to be different. And this ideal of equality leads them to the conclusion, that there should be women priests in the Catholic Church and that everybody (including non-Catholics) has the right to receive the Holy Communion and that the Church must consider the other religions as being equivalent to Catholicism. Christianity is - after liberal perception - a kind of modernized Judaism and Jewish morality is therefore largely identical with the Catholic.

The Talmudic thinking and the Talmud in general, the liberals know nothing about and they imagine that Jewish faith comes only from the Torah (= Old Testament). They imagine that the Jewish morality and philosophy of life is roughly identical to the Christians, and therefore they call the Jews "our elder brothers". They also believe, that human sexual problems are best solved using contraception and condoms and most of them think that this will be the way to solve the problem of AIDS in Africa.

Traditionalists believe that the Catholic morality differs from the Jewish and must be taken seriously. It is especially interested in the sexual norms. Here it is vital that sex outside marriage is forbidden and that Catholics are not to use artificial contraception. They are against condoms, which they do not feel are safe and which they believe helps to reduce the marital pleasure in your sex life. Marriage is intended to have children and marriages without children are more or less meaningless. Traditionalists will therefore rarely recommend marriage outside the reproductive-related perspective. It is believed that Catholic doctrine is contrary to the secular conception of equality, and it is therefore not in favor of women priests or free access for everyone to the sacraments. It is believed that the church must have an educational role for the believers, and that everyone must be willing to sacrifice and renounce his personal pleasures, to get the full benefit of the Catholic faith. Ultimately, it is those who follow the teachings and keeps the sexual bids that get the most out of life, and one therefore believes that the term "sacrifice" is a key concept, not only to understand the Mass's content, but also to understand the Catholic faith in general.

* Humanae Vitae

Liberalists are critical of all papal encyclicals, and they care especially about Humanae Vitae, which was published by Paul VI in 1968. In this encyclical, it is argued that the purpose of the Catholic marriage alone is to have children, that contraception is a sin and that the celibate life is more sacred than life in marriage.

Liberals have a hard time trying to find evidence of these views in the Bible, and especially in the common sense. They deny that the teaching of Humanae Vitae is traditional Catholic teaching, because if this was the case, then this doctrine should be found in the Eastern Orthodox Church, and that is not the case. Liberals therefore believe that Humanae Vitae is an expression of the roman church's ambitions to become a powerful institution, and therefore it sanctifies everything that helps to increase the production of children expected to become Catholics when they grow up.

When the Pope cannot convert the whole world to the Catholic faith then he tries to conquer as much as possible by ensuring the Catholic reproduction. But the ban on contraception is pure hypocrisy for the supporters of non-contraception marriages also recommend the use of the "Billing" method, which they call "natural contraception". Used in the right way, this method is claimed to be as effective as other forms of contraception, but traditionalists have difficulty explaining why believers must instead use the pill instead.

Traditionalists believe that Humanae Vitae is a very fine letter which they would like to see much more widespread, and they encourage priests to include its teaching in their sermons. They believe that the purpose of marriage is reproduction, and that this amplification is a duty and a sacrifice that marriage partners must assume. On the whole, the traditionalist worldview is much directed against marriage, which they believe is the second most holy way of life of a Catholic. Most sacred is obviously the clergy and lowest of all are those who are neither married nor priests. What such people are to be used to in the Catholic Church is an open question, but because the church claims to be open to all, they are obviously not thrown out.

* Crucifixion and Mass sacrifice

For liberals the crucifixion has no great importance. Jesus is almost a kind of moral ideal figure who taught Catholics, that one should "love your neighbor". This message, the liberals finds very enriching, and therefore they feel no need to cultivate suffering, crucifixion or the so-called Mass sacrifice. The latter refers to the Catholic notion that you are participating in the sacrifice of Jesus on Calvary, when attending the Catholic mass and thereby share in the grace and salvation that this sacrifice leads to.

For liberals, this perspective is almost scandalous, because salvation does not come through Jesus' crucifixion, but through man's own freedom of action in its own interest. The liberal priests in the church therefore warned the congregation against seeing Mel Gibson's Jesus film ("Passion of Christ", 2004), as this film particularly focused on the suffering and sacrificial aspect and even claimed (in according with the Gospels) that it was the Jews who demanded Jesus crucified. This, the liberals do not like to hear, because they feel closely connected to the Jews. Therefore they prefer other Jesus movies where the crucifixion appears in symbolic form, and the Son of God presented as moral preacher, magician and sex symbol.

Traditionalists emphasize that the Catholic faith is all about sacrifice. It is the sacrifice of Christ, who has saved the world, and it is every person's willingness to sacrifice oneself which leads to salvation. All morality is about sacrifice, and therefore there are so few who really want to profess, or to follow the Christian faith. Sacrifice of the Mass gives the faithful part in the church's accumulated moral surplus, and thus the line from Christ himself to the individual Catholic in the modern world. There is also an insurmountable contradiction between the modern world and the Catholic faith for the modern is about enjoyment and personal growth, while the Catholic faith is all about sacrifice, humiliation and following Christ. Just as Jesus sacrificed himself, we are all called to make a sacrifice. This is the only way to salvation, and that salvation can only be found in the church, not outside.

* Indulgence

Liberalists reject the whole concept of indulgences, which they believe is a remnant from the time before the Reformation. The idea that one should be able to convert the penalty for his sins to something else is wrong and absurd it becomes when the bishops and the pope distributes general indulgence for people who do one or the other piety deed such as to visit a church or attend a crusade.

Liberals believe that the church's teaching on indulgences is rooted in the need to raise money for the building of St. Peter's Basilica or other religious purposes. There is no evidence to indulgence the teachings of the Bible, and it's easy to figure out that this doctrine may seem to legitimize sin and make the believers penance in confession pure illusory. With the indulgences it is a simple matter for some people (the young, the strong and the rich) to perform the piety works that church authorities claim gives indulgence, while for others (the old, the sick and the pour), it is almost impossible. The medieval teaching that one can get indulgence by buying indulgences is therefore false and the modern teaching that you can offload some of the bishop recommended piety deeds (pilgrimage fairs, rosaries, etc.) are equally false. Not least when it is claimed that one can buy / create indulgences for other people, including the dead, whose time in Purgatory is thereby shorten. If it really is the case that God has given the Catholic bishops the right to grant absolution to people who visit certain churches and implement certain walks, he must of course love the young and healthy Europeans higher than the old and sick Africans. Is it true? Is God a racist??

Traditionalists believe that indulgences are traditional Catholic teaching, and they will gladly recommend the faithful to ensure their own salvation by investing in indulging rewarding actions whether these cost money or not. That, to go to heaven, is not only a matter of faith, but just as much a matter of ensuring that "plus point in the account" when you die. One should therefore be aware of his sins, and carried the penalty of what confession brings. Failing this, the time in purgatory is to be extended so as to avoid this it is wise to invest in indulging rewarding actions, while you still have the money and the physical ability to do it. It is the church's sacred character, its provision as "Body of Christ", which means it can distribute indulgences to the faithful, and this particular property is one of the main reasons that one must never leave the church or bring itself in conflict with its authorities. It is better to believe in something you do not understand, than it is to risk the eternal fire. It's about investing in one's own future, and the indulgence you buy for others, indirectly benefit yourself. Because one day you will get caught in the fire, and then you have to hope that there are others who will make a contribution for you to get out again.

* Relations with the Jews

Liberals believe that the positive relationship to, and imitation of the Jews, is a central aspect of the Catholic faith. They believe that Paul was wrong when he appointed Jews to be responsible for the death of Jesus and those who "*do not please God and are against all men*" (1 Thessalonians 2: 14-16). On the contrary, liberals believe that the Jews are Christians "elder brothers" and the covenant that the Jews made with God under Moses, is as valid today as it was back then. Jews did therefore not need Jesus, but Catholics, in turn, need Judaism. Therefore one celebrate the Jewish holidays and adhere to what Paul called the "Jewish myths" (Titus 1.14). These myths can be ranked, one recognizes and when they are sufficiently important they no longer call them myths. The central story that unites the liberal Jews are Hitler's Holocaust, which is so important an event that leads to prison sentences in several Catholic dominated countries, such as Germany, France, Poland and Switzerland. This liberals thinks is quite reasonable, because no faith is more important than just the belief in the Holocaust. Should a person claim that Jesus was gay or that he had never existed, it would not, however, be particularly important and it would certainly not trigger any punishment.

To retain the right to be critical of religions is essential for liberals, but this does not apply to relations with the Jewish religion, which they regard as sacred in a form that is raised over the others. The liberal Cardinal Walter Kasper from Germany said that people who do not believe in the Holocaust, are not welcome in the Catholic Church. The so-called "Holocaust deniers" is - after liberal conception - not just people with a different belief in a historical event it is people who commit a sin so great that the church cannot forgive it. Had he lived in The Middle Ages, there is little doubt that he would have suggested that they were burned.

Another liberal, the Swedish bishop Andrea Arboreliu said something similar "there is no place for such people in the Catholic Church". The church is thus regarded as a political opinion-community and not as a community of baptized and Jesus-believing people. Holocaust must, after many Jewish organizations viewpoints, be uplifted as a Catholic dogma, and the Liberals will certainly support them. Many believe that it is already the case, although it is not yet enshrined in the church's catechism. In the right perspective the crucifixion of Jesus is quite uninteresting. He was just an individual. And when his death may create as big a saving effect, then the killing of 6 million Jews must have indeed been so much greater.

The traditionalists have a more critical relationship to the Jews, who often accuse them of being "anti-Semites". As a whole traditionalists, however, share the liberals' views on the Holocaust, but they do not believe that this story has particular relevance to the Christian faith. It is believed that the church must define itself in relation to Judaism. It was the Jews who killed Jesus, and it is therefore only reasonable to retain the traditional Friday prayers at Easter for "the infidel Jews", as it sounded in the Mass before the Second Vatican Council. When one thinks that Christianity is quite different from Judaism, then one do not think that Christians must profess Jewish beliefs. The traditionalists are - generally - supporters of the people living in Europe should be allowed to examine and question the Holocaust and other historical events (e.g. 9-11), which is outside the area of the church authority to rule on. We therefore advocate freedom of expression and believe - unlike liberals - that European laws against thought crimes are contrary to Christian belief in freedom and love, and that they should therefore be repealed.

* Judeo-Catholicism

Liberals believe that the Catholic Church and its teachings are an extension of, and not a break with, Judaism. It is therefore not uncommon to members and pastors in churches with this ideology, that they call themselves Jews. The most famous example is probably the late French Cardinal Lustiger of Paris, who often pointed out that he was both Jew and Catholic, and that he believed there was no contradiction between the two religions. In Judeo-Catholic congregations, it is not unusual that the priest has the Star of David sewn on his vestments. This was the case with the catholic parish priest Georg Nibler from Lyngby. The activities one is dealing with in these congregations - in addition to the Mass - is like tourist trips to Israel and Poland (Auschwitz) and lectures by Jewish personalities of Jewish culture and world view. In such congregations they are very cautious about the use of crucifixes, especially if they are realistic, as these may shock Jewish believers. Therefore they did not develop any worship of the Virgin Mary, because this woman - after Talmudic view - certainly was no saint and far from was the Mother of God. Judeo-Catholics usually say that they are followers of the Second Vatican Council's decisions, and the document they are especially pleased about is Nostra Aetate, the declaration of the church's relationship with the non-Christian religions. Judeo-Catholics interpret this document as an end to the contradiction between Judaism and Catholic Christianity, and that is why - in their view - the Church is on a mission to integrate Judaism in the Catholic Church.

All the anti-Jewish saints and church teachers (Simon of Trient, John Chrysostom, etc.) should therefore be prohibited or forgotten and it must be made clear, that it is possible to be saved, both in this life and the next, if you are not baptized, as long as you are a part of God's covenant with the Jews. The fact that Jews can sin Judeo-Catholics do not agree about. On the one hand, they know that it is likely, but they do not like to talk about it. Sin is a Christian concept and Jews live by a completely different law.

Traditionalists believe that there is a crucial difference between Catholic and Jewish opinion. They perceive Nostra Aetate as an expression of this change in circumstances. After the 2nd World War, the church had to revise its doctrine and put it in accordance with the judgments at Nuremberg. Christianity is radically different from Judaism, and it was the Jews who were responsible for Jesus' death. Church activity, in addition to the Mass, must therefore be to develop a special Catholic spirituality and for this purpose is the rosary and adoration of the Sacrament and the Mother of God all you need.

All kinds of racism and anti-Semitism are contrary to the Catholic faith, the liberals and the traditionalists both believe, but what they put in these words, is not quite the same. For traditionalists, it is still relevant to consider Paul and the Catholic saints, which warns against the Jews. They recognize, of course, the documents from the last council, but one also believe that it is necessary to understand these documents in a historical perspective, in the same way as we see the biblical texts. Nostra Aetate is true, but the time calls for a new declaration which makes it clear that the Catholic Church has its own learning and that learning should be taken seriously.

* Holocaust

Liberals think the same way about the Holocaust as the Zionist Jews do it. This event is absolutely indisputable, and any discussion of what happened and why is in itself illegitimate. Although the word "liberal" usually is associated with the concept of freedom, then it does not apply in this context. Liberalists want to prohibit any discussion of the Holocaust, because the question - in their view - is complete. They agree with the Jewish organizations. Any doubts about the indisputable event they see as a violation of the Jews, and thus as interfering with the post-councilor Catholic faith.

They have nothing against people who believe that Jesus was gay, that the resurrection is a lie and that the Virgin Mary was a prostitute. This is ignored completely. But the same does not apply to the so-called "Holocaust deniers", who - for liberals - are all those who doubt that Hitler had gas chambers for mass killing and that the figure 6 million is historically accurate.

Traditionalists also believe in the Holocaust but recognize that there are points where one can have his doubts. For them it is about a historical event during WW2, and there is not much reason to dwell on this incident, from a Catholic perspective. Whether the Holocaust is true or not, and how it should be interpreted, is not a matter of major importance for the Christian faith, and the church has certainly no authority to determine which historical school has the most correct explanation of this incident.

Hitler was a Catholic and the same was most of his generals and the head of Auschwitz (Rudolf Höess) too, so if 6 million Jews were exterminated in gas chambers, then the Catholics hardly is without responsibility for this. The fact that Pius XII never objected to these alleged gas chambers or mass extermination overall may cause wonder and suspicion. Either this Pope was quite unusually very much under the Nazi's control, or else he was very immoral. If this does not suit, then there must be an error in logic, and I think some traditionalists reckon that there is, because they hope that Pius XII will be declared as a Catholic saint. But it will probably take some time due to the fact that the Jews are protesting, because Pius XII was partly responsible for the Holocaust, they think.

The discussion about true and false in this context can unfortunately not take place in a number of Catholic embossed countries (France, Poland etc.) because here - since the 70s - it has been decided to ban all statements that differ from Nuremberg Process results, so all of this is elevated to the sacred and eternal truth to such an extent that it leads to prison sentence to contradict it.

But everyone knows that it is the war victors who write the history. Sometime after the aftermath of WW2 have subsided there hopefully will be room to an objective discussion, both about the Holocaust and the Catholic Pope. Perhaps the truth is quite different from what the majority believe in today. The former prisoner of Auschwitz Primo Levi from Italy once said that *"what died in Auschwitz was not the Jews but the Christian faith"*. If true, it is clear that there are forces which see an advantage in keeping the demonic mythology about this camp alive. The traditionalists are aware and they want the Christian faith preserved. The whole discussion is namely, in the end, not about history. It's about what Christianity is and how Christian morality and the Christian view of humankind relate to the corresponding Jewish notions that characterize the modern world.

* Popery and the fight for "the church teaching"

The liberals do not feel bound by papal opinions or religious documents they do not understand or agree with. In the end, it is the human conscience which decides how to act and live. No matter how "infallible" the pope claims to be and no matter how much a particular theological or moral concept can be said to be rooted in church tradition, then it is only to be followed if it makes sense for the individual believer. God speaks to every human being through its conscience, so there's no reason to study ecclesiastical tradition to know God. He knows you already and you are in permanent contact with him, whether you belong to one or another religion. The idea that morality is true if it can be shown that the church and the popes previously followed this ethic can be ruled out.

If you had to preserve the past Catholic morals, you would still burn witches and you could not receive the interest from their bank deposits. It is obviously wrong. The idea that the church documents should be a comprehensive speech of God to man through its conscience, liberals consider to be Un-Catholic and false. Those who think so, are called "papists" since they apparently have more faith in the pope than the Lord of the World.

Traditionalists believe that there is something called "church teaching" and that this teaching is so unique that it can be said to be identical to the concept of "Catholic faith". This lesson can be derived from ecclesiastical documents and papal statements through the ages, and it's the Catholics duty to abide by this doctrine, if they want to be called Catholics. Alternatively, they could leave the Catholic Church, which however is not possible. The sense of belonging to this church are namely, after traditionalist view, determined by baptism, and all lawful baptized human beings are therefore Catholics, no matter if they are aware of that themselves or not. And the baptism you can't take away!

If you are dissatisfied with the Church you can send a letter to the bishop's office telling that you no longer want to be a member of the Church. Then they are erased from the member list and receive no more the church leaflets. But you are still a Catholic according to canon law.

* Conclusion

It remains to be said that there are not very many people in the Catholic Church, which uniquely claim one of those two ideologies. One cannot divide the mass participants into liberals and traditionalists, but nevertheless there is a clear difference. There are associations whose work mainly aims to promote one or the other of these ideologies, and when reading the Catholic magazines and websites, one can see that people have sympathy with, and seeks to promote views that relates to these fractions. Therefore, it is hard to be a priest (and a Pope) in the Catholic Church, because you cannot make everyone happy. If it had been in Protestant auspices, these disputes took place, thus the church would be divided. But Catholics believe that a united church is beneficial for the Christians, even if this unit is purely formal. Therefore, the conflict is sought hidden from the public, and - not least - for Catholics themselves; because the church has been broken before and it can happen again. And nobody wants that to happen.

3. POPE PIUS XII AND THE HOLOCAUST

If one follows the Vatican magazine L'Osservatore Romano and the debate between the Vatican and the Israeli state, you will find out that the question of Pope Pius XII (1876-1958) compared to the so-called Holocaust is a very hot topic. It is about something very central, not only for the state of Israel, but also to the Vatican, because there is a process underway to declare Pius XII for at saint, and if the critics of this Pope is correct in that he remained silent and ignoring what many in our time count as being Adolf Hitler's greatest crime, then Pius XII is no saint, but a criminal.

* Pope Pius XII

For both Israel and the Vatican the debate is about credibility, and nothing indicates that both parties may be right, either materially or morally. If the debate and the study of Pope Pius XII's relation to Adolf Hitler is continued, there will probably be some kind of clarification, and one of the parties will not like the result. Apparently there are only two possibilities: Either the Vatican admits that the pope, as they are in the process of declaring as a saint, is, was what we today call a "Holocaust denier", or there must be called serious questions by the historiography that since 1970 's has given the Holocaust an iconic and undeniable status.

There is no doubt about that Pius XII was against Nazism, and it is recognized by many that he did many things to protect the persecuted Jews in Italy by allowing them to seek shelter in the Vatican and in different monasteries. This is emphasized again and again by the pope's apologists, and no serious debaters will contradict them. The problem is that it is not what the debate is about, when viewed from the other side, namely Israel. This is about whether Pius XII objected to the alleged mass extermination of 6 million Jews in gas chambers at Auschwitz, Treblinka, Majdanek and Chelmno, and there is - so far - nothing that indicates that he did so. It is claimed by many western exterminist historians that Hitler's Holocaust began after holding the Wannsee Conference in January 1942, when Hitler's leaders came up with what they thought was going to be the solution to the "Jewish problem". Then started the gassings, and they continued until shortly before the Russians overtook the camps in 1945.

No one can seriously claim that Pope Pius XII did not know what happened in the Polish concentration camps. Poland is a Catholic country, there were many Catholic priests in the camps and a large part of the German staff in the camps were Catholics, including camp leader Rudolf Höess, who was a frequent visitor to the town's Catholic church. In a Catholic country like Poland, nothing can be concealed from the Catholic Church, and thus for the Pope, and beyond the intelligence that the pope got through the church channels, there also came a lot of information to the surroundings via other credible sources.

Several times Red Cross visited Auschwitz and other concentration camps, where they talked with the prisoners, and none of these visits informed about any mass executions in gas chambers. The Allies made weekly flights over Auschwitz, and they took aerial photos of the camp. But there were apparently no gas chambers to be seen, and nothing about gassing of Jews was found in the intercepted electronic communication from the camps, after the British had broken the codes. If they had received credible reports of mass executions by gas, they supposedly would have bombed the gas chambers, which would have been an easy matter, since the German air force was defeated.

It is not only Pius XII, who - apparently - did not bother to do anything to save Jews from Hitler's gas chambers. The same with President Roosevelt and Prime Minister Churchill, in whose speeches and books one searches in vain for any mentioning of the gas chambers, mass extermination and the Holocaust. On the whole, it was probably the most common perception during and after the war that Hitler had little interest in executing concentration prisoners when his goal was to force prisoners to work in the civil-war output. And the idea that he had a plan to exterminate all Jews of the world encountered the fact that Hitler never controlled land areas where more than 1/3 of the world's Jews lived. This must be added to another fact, namely that Hitler and the Nazis in the period from 1933-1940 eagerly cooperated with the Stern Gang and the other Zionists in Palestine, with the aim of getting the German Jews to go to Palestine, where they should be the core of the future state of Israel.

There is no particular reason to criticize Pius XII for not protesting against gassing and mass extermination of the Jews, because there was nobody else who did. Neither the Red Cross, the Polish priests and bishops, US President or Prime Minister of England protested, and when they did not, then it was probably because they knew nothing about such a mass extinction, or - if they had heard about it - they did not believe in it.

Among the arguments that the Vatican has made to clean Pius XII of the accusations of the moral co-responsibility in the alleged mass extermination of 6 million Jews, it is that everything would have been much worse if the Pope had protested. When using this argument the defenders of Pius XII implicitly admit that he had knowledge of systematic mass extermination, but he chose to keep quiet, not to provoke the offender to do something even more horrifying.

But this argument does not hold. Firstly, it is difficult to see how a crime can be any greater than what it is claimed that Hitler committed and which since the 70s has achieved iconic status and is referred to in movies and history books under the term Holocaust (with a capitalized first letter). If the Pope was in favor of a moral principle not to protest against evil "not to make it worse," then it's hard to understand why he several times - before and after the war - protested against Communist oppression of the Catholic Church in the Russian controlled countries. In that case he should also have kept quiet about this, not to "provoke the oppressors." But he did not. Moreover, it has never been Catholic morality not to protest against the evils to prevent them from being worse of "doing the worse", at such an intent can hardly apply to Pius XII, especially since his silence on the alleged extermination continued after the end of the war and until his death in 1958.

What Pius XII was can nowadays be named as a "Holocaust denier" the only plausible explanation for his silence is that he simply did not believe the stories that today have become a historical dogma, which does not tolerate debate or contradiction. Although the postulated mass extinction was the basis for judgments at Nuremberg trial, there was no one who took them quite seriously. It is always war winners who write history and the purpose of this trial was to stigmatize the losers as being immoral. It succeeded. Since American NBC in 1978 produced a television series in four parts entitled Holocaust, this concept become a central theme in all discussion of WW2. There is hardly a major US or European city that does not have a Holocaust museum, and we can daily watch TV shows where we are taught that the Holocaust was the central and moral watershed event in WW2. It is because of the Holocaust, that Hitler today is thought of being a psychopath and war criminal, while his opponents are idealized and regarded as heroes.

The concept of the Holocaust has today taken an iconic status, and there are reasons for why the former Catholic (now Muslim) Roger Geraudy calls one of his books "The foundational myth of Israel". Geraudy takes no position on the historical reality of the Holocaust story, but just notes that this story has achieved a religious status, and serves today as the basic ideological pinpoint for the state of Israel, and to some extent for the entire Western world. It is therefore in all so-called democratic Western countries allowed to ridicule and violate both Jesus and Muhammad, and - of course - to raise doubts about their historical existences. But at the same time one will go to jail for example in Germany and France if you indicate that you do not believe in the historical reality of the Holocaust.

It is therefore correct to describe the Western post-Christian culture as being a holocaust culture, since this concept - and not in Christianity - has the untouchable core of what the citizens of the United States and Europe believe. To deny the historical realities behind the Holocaust, is leading to the same kind of sanctions that were once triggered in the Middle Ages, if you expressed doubts about the Trinity or - as Galilei - claimed the truth, that the earth rotated around the sun.

Freedom of expression stops when there is a particular religion which is violated. It does not matter for the others. Just like Muslims cannot tolerate violations of the Prophet, the Western Judaized human do not tolerate doubt on the Holocaust. And the Catholic Church follows suit. Admittedly, some claim that they are in favor of free speech, but when Catholics are imprisoned in Germany and France for denying the Holocaust, then the church remains silent.

* Israel's occupation

Israel has full support in the US and in Denmark. Racism and colonialism is something abhorrent when it takes place in South Africa, but in Palestine it is quite in order. The logic is simple: The occupation and terror in Palestine is done by the "Holocaust survivors", and they cannot be subjected to moral rules. When there is a war between Jews and Palestinians, it is the Jews who are "victims", even if they are the ones who have occupied Palestinian land.

I think that Israel is going to win the debate with the Vatican on Pius XII. Not because they are right, but because they control the media in the United States who obviously supports Israel. In the spring of 2007 the Vatican's ambassador to Israel threatened to boycott a memorial in the Israeli Holocaust museum, Yad Vashem and the reason was that they could not tolerate the Israeli interference in the canonization process of Pius XII. But the Vatican is to blame for its problems. They believe in the Hollywood promoted version of the Holocaust, and therefore no excuses saves Pius XII from being morally complicit in the mass extermination of Jews.

One understands the Vatican frustrations and all their bad explanations about why the pope did not protest against the Holocaust. Their claims, that he did not protest "for not doing the oppression worse" or because he "did not know what happened" is obviously false. The Pope knew better than anyone what happened in Poland. It was his subjects, who performed the work in the camps, regardless of what this work so consisted in.

So there are only two possibilities:

1. Either the extermination of 6 million Jews in the Polish gas chambers is a historical reality, thus Pius XII knew of it. A gigantic crime could not possibly be hidden from him and the pope was therefore - through his silence - morally co-responsible for 6 million human's deaths.

2. Or else, we must recognize that the NBC story about the Holocaust is not quite identical to what happened in the real world.

The conclusion can only be the one that either Pius XII was a Holocaust-denier and a morally decaying individual. Or the reality is that he did not believe the stories of gassings or mass extinction in the German concentration camps. Therefore he did not protest.

But if the pope knew about the mass extermination of millions of Jews, despite the fact that he had better information than any other person in the world, how could they take place? There is no doubt that one has their own answer to this question in Israel and the Vatican. It's about honor. Either the Israeli ideology is built on historical falsehood and mythology or Pius XII was a Holocaust denier and morally a criminal. Israel and the Vatican cannot both be right.

5. IS THE POPE INFALLIBLE?

At the First Vatican Council in 1870 the Catholic Church adopted one of its most disastrous dogma, namely the doctrine that the Roman Pope - if he wants it - can claim that he speaks infallibly "ex. cathedra" when he states on issues concerned with theology or morality.

The purpose of the adoption of this dogma was to increase the authority of the Pope and thereby counter the modernist currents that characterized the church in the late 1800s. One must remember that it is not possible to throw members out of the church, since membership of the Catholic Church is based on baptism, and even the Pope cannot take baptism from a human. The church therefore need another instrument to keep discipline in the ranks to avoid endless, exhausting discussions about issues such as women priests, shared communion, universalism etc.

There are an endless number of questions that Catholics can discuss with each other and most of these discussions will have the result that you end up having two or more different opinions and their advocates that cannot agree. Therefore, the church needs a Magisterial, which can take decisions and thereby force the necessary discipline needed to avoid the church to split and new fractions to arise believing that the church is wrong in this or the other way.

There are currently 1.2 billion Catholics across the globe and the reason the church has been able to keep unified, despite this diversity, is that there exists a powerful Magisterial. So it is understandable that they had hoped for this dogma. But in the light of rational thought and Christian theology, the dogma is a disaster. First, a person or a dogma is not infallible just because a Church assembly claims that he is. Assemblies are wrong again and again, and this also applies when these assemblies are ecclesiastical councils. If the adoption of an ecclesiastical council on papal infallibility is to be valid, it must be the premise that this council also is infallible. And the consequence of this is that all councils in church history have been infallible, including the councils, which in the Middle Ages chose three simultaneous popes, which for decades fought each other about who was the real pope.

As councils consist of people (bishops) who makes decisions, then does the idea that the Councils are infallible. If the council is infallible, then the bishops present in this council must be infallible too. And so it goes on. When everything is summed up, then the infallibility dogma entails the entire church, all the popes, all its councils and all its priests. They all are infallible. The church and its staff have therefore - as a consequence of this - never made mistakes!

From a church perspective, this view might make sense, but it does not make sense from the perspective of the believer's and from the perspective of the other world religions. History shows many examples of Catholic priests who have made wrong decisions and ecclesiastical decisions that have been damaging. But of course you can decide that all this is just a sinful world blindness for "God's perfection", which it works in the church and among its employees. In such cases, the Reformation, which was performed by disobedient Catholic bishops and priests are also infallible Catholic teaching on homosexuality is infallible, the numerous pedophile abuse is infallible and the three warring popes were also infallible.

No one can prevent a church - or people in general - to declare themselves as infallible. At institutions of insanity there are usually people who think they are God, or that their actions are directed by God. And it's hard to disprove that people are guided by God if they believe in it themselves.

But the world has learned to be careful when such God-apostles are trying to assert themselves. We must remember that the Muslim conquest of the Middle East and the Muslim actions to liquidate the Christian churches everywhere in the Islamic dominant countries also happens "in the name of God". On the whole, there is probably not a criminal in the world who has not used the name of God to

34

justify his actions, so that people in general are fortunately so reasonable that they are very critical of such statements. The Catholic Church's teaching that its popes, councils, and thus the entire church are infallible, is not only untrustworthy and against historical experience. It also helps to make a fool out of the church.

5. DOES MARY HAVE A FREE WILL?

Among the very unfortunate doctrines that the "infallible" popes have adopted, the Pius IX's dogma from 1854 about Virgin Mary being born without original sin is one of the most unfortunate. The reason behind this dogma is probably the same as behind the slightly late adoption of the idea that Pope could speak infallibly. It was about that the church was in a crisis that had to do with the development of the modern era and the nascent socialism, which contradicted church teaching in almost all areas.

The church needed more authority, and since we know that the Virgin Mary is one of the most popular characters in the hierarchy of saints, the Church chose to increase this woman's theological and moral status by declaring that she was "born without original sin." It had for centuries been the church's belief that the Virgin Mary had not sinned even once in her entire life, but now the trump is played, that she did not even had the opportunity to sin, for all sin in Christian theology is derived from original sin. So who has no original sin, is not able to sin.

But what are the consequences of this dogma?

After all, if the Virgin Mary was born without original sin, so is the inevitable consequence that she was incapable of sinning. Unlike all the other people who can sin and who actually sins then she could not do so. She therefore had no free will, as ordinary people, but was a kind of robot that can only do good, and not evil. And when a human being cannot do evil, then there is no reason to praise this person for not doing evil, because you can only praise a person to act in a certain way, if this person had the opportunity to act differently. If you are forced to do any good then this is in fact - morally - not good at all, because moral virtues presuppose that man has a free choice. And this, the pope did not believe, that the Virgin Mary had.

The situation is comparable to if it was discussed to appoint an ambulance (a car) as saint, because this car has been of great help saving many people from dying" But this makes no sense. An ambulance, a car, a physical object that has no free will, and that one cannot therefore have moral attitudes. We can discuss whether the people who run the ambulance makes it good or not, but the ambulance itself is completely without moral qualities. It is a machine that does what it is designed to do, namely to drive sick people to the hospital.

Similarly, it makes no sense to declare the Virgin Mary as a good person, if she did not have a free will and thus the possibility of acting differently from the way she did. Then she was a robot, and robots are neither morally good nor evil, just as an ambulance is not good or bad. The consequence of the papal statement on the Virgin's unique lack of original sin is thus that the church's greatest saint was not an ordinary person and therefore not a figure that other ordinary people can reflect themselves on. She may not any longer be an inspiration to those who want to do any good, because she cannot be compared to these people, since she did not have original sin. She is - in the Roman theology - a lofty icon, a beautiful face, a work of art and a lovely fantasy. She is not a real woman of flesh and blood, which we all can reflect ourselves in.

6. WHEN BENEDIKT XI ABOLISHED CHRISTIANITY

As everyone knows, the Christian faith is associated with the faith of the Holy Trinity, Jesus' deity, baptism necessity and the possibility of salvation in the life hereafter. The now abdicated German Pope Benedict XI started his career under the name Joseph Ratzinger and worked as a professor of theology. One must therefore assume that he was aware of these concepts that are central elements in the Catholic religion.

But to understand Pope Benedict XI one should probably understand his background and his origins. Benedict was German and he had during WW2 been a soldier in Hitler's army. He had been in the struggle against Hitler's enemies and one must assume that he identified himself more or less with his employer, as he struggled. He certainly did not desert and did not participate in resistance work or attempt to overthrow Hitler or promote the racist regime's collapse. He was an obedient and loyal soldier, just like most others. How many Russian and allied soldiers he killed, no one knows.

When Ratzinger was elected Pope, there were many who feared the worst, because it is a known fact that Germany and its people still suffer from war trauma and always were trying to do everything they could to convince the world that they were "not Nazis anymore." Judging by the contents of the recent American and English film, it is not yet succeeded to any great extent. In every James Bond film and many other popular movies, you use the Germanic appearance and the German accent as sure indication that a person is evil and has nefarious intentions. Perhaps that is why that in Germany they do not show these movies with the original sound, but choose to dub them, to make them more "understandable" for the German audience.

Pope Benedict was never quite sure that he had convinced the skeptical outside world that he entirely had left his youthful conviction and had become a true Catholic, which (acc. Catechism) i.e. 100 % opponent of racism, nationalism, anti-Semitism and genocide. It would take more.

And Benedict took the opportunity to show his Catholic purity and his showdown with anti-Semitism since the English traditionalist bishop Richard Williamson declared (in a Swedish TV broadcast) that he did not believe that Hitler had had homicidal gassings of Jews and that he did not believe the story of the 6 million Jews who were alleged to have been gassed in those gas chambers.

Williamson was what one in Germany calls "Holocaust denier" and that kind is prohibited in Germany, which over the past 60 years has paid war reparations to Israel and are still struggling to convince its Jewish friends about that now it is of a completely different mindset than what dominated the 30's.

The Pope immediately called a number of Jewish organizations from the United States to a meeting at the Vatican, where he assured them that "you cannot be Catholic, if you do not believe in the Holocaust." And the same Gospel, one could hear in the press that a few German cardinals repeat, so now it was quite clear. You cannot be Catholic, if you do not believe in the Holocaust!

The problem is that the Holocaust is not mentioned in the Bible or in the Catholic catechism with a single word, so it must be said that these books - which the church has edited - are very misleading. One can understand the editors of the Bible, whose first edition was published about 450 after Christ and 1500 years before WW2. But what about the Catholic Catechism with its many clauses and doctrines to explain the Catholic believer on what they should believe. How can such an oversight have sneaked into this document?

If the Holocaust is the fundamental dogma that Catholics must believe in, then you have to expect it to be mentioned in the church's catechism, which is a fundamental textbook for all Catholics. But Holocaust is not even mentioned in the catechism or in any of the

Church resolutions made on the 2nd Vatican Council (1962-65).
Why?

The conclusion must be, that either Pope Benedict XI is a liar or the
Church is based on deception. There are no other options. Because
if people are invited to join the Catholic Church to pay their money
to the church to seek salvation, then one must expect that this
church honestly tells what the Catholic faith is. And they don't do
that. If the Catholic faith has the Holocaust as an essential dogma,
then it must be made clear to the believers. So it must be made
clear in church documents and doctrines. But it is not. The Holocaust is not mentioned with a single word. Neither Council Decla-
rations, in the Catholic Catechism or in the "Catholic Mini-
dictionary" published here in Denmark around 1990.

Who is right, Benedict XI or the Catechism? They cannot both be
right, because they contradict each other. To the old Nazi Pope this
might not matter. His real employers live in Israel and he has problems with his conscience. I understand him, but I do not sympathize
with him. For him the faith in Holocaust is the basics. I will not call
him a Christian and he can only be commended for one thing,
which he did: He withdrew. He could not continue his acting!

7. CATHOLIC EXPERIENCES

* Introduction

In 1995 I was fully initiated in the Catholic Church, as they call it. I should perhaps never have been, but I really had no choice. I have always been interested in religion, but I preferred to be free in relation to the religion that I studied, partly, because I perceive religions as ideological systems which - like other systems - have their limitations, and partly, because I do not like to apply new religion's names to me. Partially due to that reason, I decided to sign out of the Lutheran church when I was 19 years old.

Basically there is only one name that I can really identify with, and that is that I am a culture sociologist. I am proud of that and I am satisfied with it. This designation gives a good idea of who I am and what I am interested in. Because culture is norms, ideology and religion, and one of the most obvious topics of cultural social studies are the religions.

There are also other things about the sociology of culture, which I like, and that is the critical attitude to everything, and the lack of respect for authority. I can totally identify with this. Authorities are found in all cultures, because they cannot be dispensed without, but for us the culture sociologists, these authorities are not of infallible sizes which one yields to, but - in itself - objects of our study. This does the skilled authorities not mind, while the less skilled balk. They know that their authority is false and they fear detection. I have learned this through my working years as a course instructor for many companies, and this was also my experiences in the Catholic Church too. Authority is everywhere, but not all places in a positive manner.

Well, back to the big day, when I joined the church. I had for many years studied religion, and as my life evolved such that I felt the need for even to belong to such a religion, so I focused my quest against this. Not because that affiliation with a religion provides social contacts, but more because that religion is a way to understand and to speak of the divine and the afterlife. And this was something I needed. I had in fact lost a large part of my family (my son, my sister and my dad) and I felt that I needed a spiritual foundation. But what religion this should be I knew nothing about. So I spent time and effort to learn about the different systems of thought, and I knew I was baptized and lived in a Christian country, so I thought it would be wise to choose one of the Christian religions.

I therefore visited a lot of Christian churches to find out what they stood for. I also read a lot of books and talked with many people who had an opinion about the religious. In a few months I was a member of the Unitarian faith communities in Copenhagen, as I felt that the concept of the Unitarian God sounded very sensible. Why I felt such, I do not remember, but I discovered that there were numerous unresolved issues in the Unitarian assembly and that I in some crucial areas was in contrast to the majority of its members. I was such an opponent of abortion, I did not believe in reincarnation and I did not think you could base a religion on several conflicting "holy books" at one time. So on this basis, I find that Unitarianism was not the right thing for me, and together with a friend who I had met at the Unitarians, I therefore started a group which we called the "Christian Unitarians".

The group was never extended with other members other than her and me, but it was only an advantage. Thus we got: access to the inter-religious cooperation, which at the time took place in Copenhagen between a number of associations of Christian and non-Christian kind, and this collaboration I learned a great lot from. After this study of the many religions that exists in Denmark, it was clear to me that a religion has to have some solid frames. There must be a minimum of consensus on what it contains. If you do not agree on what is sacred writings, when life begins, who are priests, and what is the goal of life, one must expect that there will be conflicts, and these conflicts will - sooner or later - lead to splitting up.

It was my opinion that the most serious religion and the one who had a doctrine that was closest to what I already believed, was the Catholic religion. I actually grew up near a Catholic Church (Sct. Andreas) in Ordrup (close to Copenhagen) and had been involved with Catholics and Catholic priests most of my youth. What appealed to me in the Catholic religion, was that it was international, it was old, it had many members (especially abroad), it had a strict theology and it had a positive view of humanity and it believed in the existence of the free will.

Especially the latter played a big role to me, because I have always considered it obvious that people are responsible for their own actions. The very thought that God should judge his own creations for "faith without deed", which Luther thought, seemed to me to be completely insane and utterly immoral. If God loves His children in this world, he must give them the freedom to choose, and he must - like other sensible parents - make these children realize that their actions have consequences. One should not go to heaven if you do not deserve it, because before you go to heaven there is a judgment, and this judgment makes no sense if everyone goes the same way. Therefore, man cannot be without free will, because then the judgment makes no sense. And then God is unjust.

The Calvinist teaching that our destiny is predetermined, or the Lutheran idea that our actions always will be evil and that our will is enslaves, is totally unacceptable to me. It can surprise me that religions with such a philosophy exist at all. Although I am in favor of free speech, but to make a view of humanity as the Lutheran state religion in a Denmark does, seems to me to be sick. I took strong exception to this and I still do.

My studies led me to the conclusion that the most serious church I could become a member of, was the Catholic. But I had no experience with this church, beyond the fact that several of my playmates as a child, were Catholics. But what this meant, I had not thought about, and my parents had never tried to influence me in a religious direction. I was therefore free to choose, I knew, and I thought that the best choice I could do was to initiate a closer study of the Catholic Church, with regards to joining.

* Apprenticeship and initiation

My study of the Catholic Church started, when I borrowed some videos in the Catholic video library. It was an older Jesuit pastor named pater Dorn, who was responsible for this library, and he seemed very sympathetic to me. The videos I borrowed were perhaps not very interesting, but on the other hand, they did not frighten me away, so I decided to continue the search. I did this by contacting the Catholic bishop's office where I asked to get an interview with a Catholic priest, and here I was referred to a Jesuit priest who lived in Frederiksberg, not far from my home. Also he was quite older than me, which I liked. I visited him a few times and it was always interesting to talk to him, but I understood, that he did not have the time to talk more to me. He therefore referred me to a younger priest, who lived in an apartment on the Gammel Kongevej in Copenhagen, but him I was not fond of. He seemed supercilious and self-righteous, so I did not want anything to do with him.

My next step was to contact the Catholic information service led by a sister Hildegaard. I called her and I was told that I could sign up for a Catholic correspondence course in 10 lessons. It would be quite free, and if I was further interested, then I could get personal lessons. I therefore started with the Catholic corresponding course, and continued with private lessons at the respective sister, and everything I learned here I found very interesting and in full conformity with the position that I already had. The key point for me was that the Catholics believe that life is sacred, abortion is prohibited and that man has a free will. Sin exists and it has to do with the way you live life. God does not judge people by "faith alone", but after the way we relate to others and the sacrifices we make for our fellow human beings. This was how I understood what she told me, and it was completely in line with my own views. At the same time,

I also got a clearer understanding of what Lutheranism was, and it was quite clear to me that this religion - Lutheranism - was completely out of line with the God that I believed in.

After attending classes at sister Hildegaard in half a year she asked me if I "would to become a Catholic." I must admit that I was not surprised by this question, but I also knew that it would be a difficult choice. I was in fact not fully agreeing with the church's official positions on various issues (e.g. contraceptives and indulging), and when I thought it unlikely that I would be able to influence the church to change its teachings, I thought I had to make reservations. But Sister Hildegaard lined it starkly up to me. Either the teaching should be aiming towards that I joined the church, or she had no more time for me. This I understood, and when I thought that the teaching was very valuable to me, I chose therefore the "least worse" of these alternatives, namely that I wanted inclusion in the church.

It must be said that already from the beginning of the teaching I had made it clear to my teacher that I did not agree with the papal teaching about contraceptives. She had fully accepted this, and it was my impression that she agreed with my views in this area. At least she did not try to convince me of something else, which she would probably have done if she had disagreed. And now she asked me if I wanted to become a Catholic. I hesitated.

In return, she asked me if I would finish what now suddenly was called my "convert-education" with her, or if I wanted another teacher. It was a difficult question, because sister Hildegaard was interesting to talk to. But I thought anyway that I would be better off if I also learned something from other Catholics than sister Hildegaard before I was initiated to the church, so I asked to have another teacher who could take me all the way to the final initiation in the church. I told her that this teacher should preferably be a Jesuit pater called Dorn, whom I knew from the Catholic video central, where I had seen several of the videos they were distributing. I liked him. But Sister Hildegaard told me that it was not possible because Father Dorn had so much to do that he did not have time to teach converts. So I had to find another teacher.

My further search was through the Danish Catholic register where I found the name and telephone number of a number of Catholic institutions that I wanted to become more familiar with. This led to some interesting visits and conversations with people who all taught me something. At one time I talked with Jesuit Father in Stenosgade, and he invited me to go to lessons with him, which. But the Pater was certainly not a type that I felt inspired by. He seemed angry and stubborn, and he was not able to respond even moderately convincing to the questions that I asked. When I asked him what he thought of indulgences, he just gave me a photocopy of a dictionary, where the concept was defined. But I did not get any wiser, and therefore I informed him shortly after that I did not want to continue the teaching.

My last teacher was George Bune Andersen, and he was the leader of an association called Catholic Workers Action. I called him to arrange a visit, as I had done with several other Catholic layman movements. But Bune Andersen did not just answer my questions, he also asked questions, and when I told him that I was a convert student without a teacher, he asked if I would like to go for training with him. My desire was, I told him, to be a student of Father Dorn, but because Father Dorn did not have the time, Bune Andersen could be a good substitute. Especially since he said he worked closely with Father Dorn and that he lived right next to the Jesuit's Dormitory, where Father Dorn lived. I did therefore said "yes" to Bune Andersen's offers, thus assuming that Father Dorn would approve it, and he did.

I was then a so-called "indirectly" student of Dorn and my admission in the church would be made by Father Dorn. However, it would be Bune Andersen, who was in charge of my education up until the initiation. I think that sounded reasonable, and I immediately started the lessons.

It was a glorious time. George Bune Andersen was anything but dogmatic, and he had roots in the socialist labor movement, which I had also had contact with for several years. Until 1979 I had been member of the Communist Party and of the Communist student movement. Bune Andersen and I therefore had much to talk about, and the way he connected the Catholic Church with the labor movement and the struggle for social justice, made a great impression on me. I did not agree with him on everything. I found, inter alia, out that the association he chaired, had campaigned for abortion, and I could certainly not accept this. But in other areas, we fully agreed. None of us thought that the papal "infallibility" was something that had to be taken too literally, and the fact that God communicates to each person through this person's conscience (not through the Catholic Pope) we were also completely agreeing. The church is a cultural institution which many can enjoy, and the people who lead this institution are no more infallible than any other. And it means very little.

Bune Andersen was prepared to accept that I soon should be initiated in the church, and I was convinced that if Catholics in general were just as inspiring and easy-going as him, then I would not have any problems. What nagged me the most was the formula that you have to recite, when you joined the church; part of that creed sounds like this:

> *"I believe and profess all that the Catholic Church teaches, as revealed by God."*

I thought that this could be interpreted in two ways, and I could only endorse one of these interpretations. I did not believe that anything the Catholic Church has learned has been revealed by God. The church and the popes once taught the believers that witches and heretics should be burnt and that the sun revolved around the earth and that cremation was forbidden. This nonsense I naturally could not agree on. For me it was love, forgiveness and justice, which was the core of the Christian religion, and my interest in the Catholic Church, was based on the belief that they thought the same. I had no sympathy for unexplainable moral standards, so if that phrase should have any meaning, it had to be interpreted in such a way that that I had to believe everything revealed by God. Since this revelation ended when the last apostle died (about 100 years after the birth of Christ) it could obviously not be about the whole church's teaching, which for the most part was developed after this time.

As a precaution, I took reservations when I joined the church. When I delivered the said phrase, I made a mental reservation. Only if the sentence was in the sense that I could accept, I'd believe it. This reservation makes me happy today, because it means that I never have had to compromise on behalf of my conscience. Even in the Catholic context.

I discovered later on that the traditionalists and Papists, that the hierarchy is filled with, always used the argument of "church teaching" when they do not have any factual arguments left in a debate. But here I was fortunately immune. Because I had never acknowledged the belief that everything that the church teaches is revealed by God. Of course, this is not the case, and one must wonder why they require the converting student to take such a confession, to be able to get access to the sacraments. I wonder why that is? I have an idea, but I will keep it to myself.

* The new bishop

The first distrust of the church's hierarchy arose in me, when the old Bishop Martensen was permitted to retire and the Vatican chose the young Czeslaw Kozon to be the new bishop. I did not know Kozon in advance, but did know, that he had practiced as priest at the Church in Ordrup, not far from where I had lived in my youth. I was told that he had been good in respect to dealing with young people, and that he was considerably more conservative than his predecessor. The last did not sound very good in my ears, when I considered myself as being liberal, and taught by my experiences from political life and from the jobs I have had, I realized that I did not function well during an authoritarian leadership.

Bishop Kozon who I met the first time, when he walked around the yard on St. Lioba monastery in Frederiksberg, where my first converts teacher lived. It was the day of anointing of the sick, and there were some guests. Here he handed out fliers that showed a picture of Saint Ansgar, who was carrying a church, and on the back of these notes it said: "Pray for me. Czeslaw Kozon". What was the purpose of these notes I had the difficulty of understanding, because he had just been appointed bishop, and thus had all the power he could imagine for himself. Was there no other, who was more appropriate to pray for, I thought? And you could not use the diocesan money on some better ways than to print advertisements for the bishop? I wondered, and thought what might be the next thing? For it was clear that the shift to the new bishop would not only be a person change but also a change in leadership, morale and atmosphere throughout the diocese. The new bishop was from Poland, but was raised in Denmark. He spoke Danish and was a Danish citizen, but was in all ways otherwise - according to the information I had received - utterly un-Danish.

The first reform as the new bishop had launched was to sack the former editor of the diocesan magazine, Catholic Orientation. It happened at the request of some conservative laymen, who thought that he was too critical and liberal. The bishop appropriated money so they could make a major survey of the magazine's editorial line. The most prominent laymen who supported the "neoconservative revolution" were Sebastian Olden-Jørgensen and Erling Tidemann, two of the people who would later become major beneficiaries of the new bishop and his leadership. The old editor was fired and instead they employed priest and psychologist Jørgen Hviid, to serve as a transitional figure before Erling Tidemann - a most conservative layman - could take over.

The changes in the editorial management had obviously not only intended to reward the people who supported the bishop, it was also about learning the Danish Catholics to think in a new way. It was especially their attitude to the relationship between their conscience on one side and the papal teaching on the other, which the new bishop wanted to change. The Catholic member's morality should not be ruled by the expression of God's voice in their conscience, but by the ecclesiastical tradition, as it was expressed in the papal encyclicals. Especially one of them had an interest, namely Paul VI's letter "Humanae Vitae" of 1968. The Nordic bishops (incl. Hans Martensen) had taken the distance indirectly from this encylical when it was published´, but things had changed. Now Catholic morality was revised. It should be made clear that the issues of contraception and cohabitation could not be determined by the people for their own subjective assessment, but had to be arranged by the church's "infallible" teachings: Contraception and masturbation was a sin, homosexuality was a sin, sex outside of marriage was a sin, short said all erotic activity without the purpose of having children was a sin. The idea was that the main purposes of the church is to increase its own membership, and all experiences shows that converts are unreliable, so one needs to focus on the Catholics who are born of Catholic parents and baptized in the Catholic Church.

Converts are the people who have changed their mind, and who at one point - subjectively - have chosen the Catholic faith. They will just as easily choose another religion, and therefore they are considered unstable. Real Catholics must be born of Catholic parents, and therefore such spouses adjust to the fact that they must have many children. One of the bishop's most vigorous proponents was therefore the chairman of a Catholic association against abortion. Torben Riis was his name, and he did not neglect an opportunity to advertise in the papal sexual doctrine and its ban on contraception. He himself had 10 children, so he was a man of the kind that the bishop liked. Therefore he was also - after Erling Tidemann - appointed as editor of Catholic Orientation.

In addition to the change of the Catholic magazine, there was also many other changes that pointed in the same direction, namely towards authoritarian leadership, personality cult, traditionalism and

Popery (= uncritically Pope-belief). In the Catholic cathedral was the closet with the Sacrament ("the body of Jesus") moved from the center of the apses and out to a side wall, to which instead should be room for the bishop's throne, which was a red, velvet-covered chair. When the church guests looked ahead they should look at the bishop and not at the body of Christ. And the chair might of course be used only by the bishop, who was rarely seen anywhere in the church, without wearing his Bishop's cape. There was no doubt that Bishop Kozon wanted to emphasize his authority, as being "one of the successors of the apostles," but the content of this authority was less clear. I remember that one day I came past the bishop's office in Bredgade, and the door was open. I looked in and wondered why there was hanging a photo of the bishop himself on the wall. The most important for the office guests was apparently to know what the bishop looked like. A crucifix might have been more appropriate, I thought, but it was obviously not of the bishop's opinion. It was obvious the idea, that we had to focus on him as a person, much like an idol. And I did not like that. The return to old values can be a good thing, but unnecessary highlighting empty authority, I do not consider appropriate. The bishop seemed like a man who appealed to yes-men; a man for those who like authority, obedience and absence of personal responsibility, a man for whom conscience only speaks in validity if it was in accordance with the Pope's words, and thus a man who I did not like.

In addition to the above, there were also other changes. The bishop moved from a humble vicarage attached to a local Catholic Churceh into a large mansion in a very expensive location called Hellerup. The price of this mansion I do not know, but tens of millions kroner is probably a realistic guess. And it's only fair, the bishop has probably thought, because he is the local "Vicar of Christ", so he should have e prestigious house to live in. Amalienborg - the castle of our Queen - had probably been a more suitable address, but there was apparently nothing available. Therefore the bishop had to settle for a mansion in Hellerup. We know that poverty and modesty are virtues, which Jesus values highly and the church also claim to believe in. But it is apparently not these values that the bishop chose his mansion after. Double standards it is called, but what does it do? Catholics confess in every mass that they have "*sinned in thought, word and deed.*" And then you are probably also obliged to do it in practice. At least if you are a bishop.

* Personal matters

In my early years in the church, I learned a lot, not at least through some individual cases which I became acquainted with when I knew the people who it was about. The first case concerned a person named Bent Wilson, who had been accepted into the church at the same time as me. We had been at the convert's course together at Magleås and we both belonged to the Heart of Jesus Church in Copenhagen. Bent Wilson was an enterprising gentleman who claimed he was a lawyer and former director of a major company in the US. He said that he had finished his career and that he had returned to Denmark while he was converted to the Catholic faith. Now would he use his skills to help poor children in the streets of Saint Petersburg, and for this purpose he founded the Aid Association "Petri Help", which the local pastor Sanders in the Heart of Jesus Church was kind enough to provide shelter.

Unfortunately it turned out after a year that all the money that the Petri Help had collected had mysteriously disappeared, and the rumor said that the association's leader was not quite the person he himself had stated. Instead of being a former director of an American company, he had been sitting in the Vestre Prison, convicted of fraud. The man had apparently concluded that the Catholic Church was a favorable place for him to continue his fraud, and he was probably right in this perspective. Several requests from myself and others to the local parish priest and bishop Kozon, gave no result. The bishop visited the parish council, but found nothing wrong in their work, and this despite the fact that one of the church members had initiated a private lawsuit against Mr. Wilson. The problem was, unfortunately, the parish council members to some extent was implicated in the fraud, and therefore the whole thing did not end before they even became victims of Wilson's scams. One day you could read in the church magazine that Mr. Wilson was no longer a member of the parish council, and that they did not anymore support his so called aid association. There had been money mislaid from the ward council's own account, which no one liked. They therefore informed the church members about Mr. Wilson's factual background which they had always known, but which you had kept hidden from the people whom he had deceived. All of this in the name of "love".

But now it was all over. At this time, Wilson had cheated a few hundred thousand DKK, but the case was never fully resolved. The police in Copenhagen refused to investigate it because it "had happened internally in a Catholic church," and therefore they did not want to interfere. "People can just stay away," said the police officer from Vesterbro Police, who I talked to, and he was probably right.

The other interesting individual case, which I was involved in, was when the chairman of the parish council in Sacrament Church was ex-communized in 1997. After my experiences in the Heart of Jesus Church, I had resolved parish band and was now assigned to Sacrament Church, and that I had met Flemming the chairman of the parish board. He had been married for many years, but his wife was dead, and then he met a divorced Protestant woman who he had moved in with. The woman seemed that the Catholic Church was exciting, and she joined Flemming to Mass every Sunday, where she - with the pastor's permission - received Holy Communion. But some of the others in the congregation was not happy about that, and they threatened to complain to the new bishop. The priest therefore no more dared to provide the divorced lady Communion, and that made Flemming very angry. But the problem was not really serious before the time that he and his girlfriend married in a Protestant church. They could not be joined in matrimony in a Catholic church, so the alternative would be the town hall, or a Protestant church, and they chose the latter. Therefore the priest told Flemming that he was no longer welcome to receive Communion, and that made Flemming so angry that he left the Catholic Church. When his new wife died a few years later, he could have returned, but he did not. The anger was too great and he felt no more that he belonged to the Catholic community.

The third individual case, which I could not fail to relate to, was about a friend of mine, from my time in the Communist movement. His name was Martin Bergsøe and he had been a student of Nordic Literature at the University of Copenhagen while he was an active member of the Communist student movement. In fact, he was so active that he was granted a special education at a party school in Moscow, because he was seen to be one of the future men in the Communist Party. I knew him from the main board of the communist student unions, where we both had been members.

Martin Bergsøe's development was not totally different from my own. At one point he left the communist movement, and in the search for a different standpoint, he had found the Catholic Church. Not in the sense that communism and Catholicism is the same, but on the other hand, there are certain distinctive features which they have in common. They are international movements, they have an ideology and a central leadership, and they claim to be the start of the ultimate community. Communists call it *communism* and Catholics for *Communion*. The methods are different, but the goal is - as I saw it - roughly the same.

But there were differences between Martin and me. When I was accepted into the Catholic Church, there were several who encouraged me to become a priest. I had refused because I did not think that I would feel comfortable in an authoritarian environment that the Catholic Church is known for. The same decision Martin did not come to, and it was perhaps a mistake. He had - more or less on his own account - initiated a priest study in Rome and later he was ordained as a Catholic priest. Everywhere I went in the Catholic Church, I heard that they were fond of him. Especially the women, who usually represents between 60 and 80 % of the Catholic congregations, could tell that he was just a type that they liked, and during my visits to his congregation in Taastrup I had seen that the enthusiasm was mutual. Martin liked women. It did not surprise me very much, when I heard that Martin was moved in with one of his former parishioners, a pretty girl who came from a Catholic family. But this did unfortunately made his work as a Catholic priest impossible, and therefore he left the church, and joined a biblical fundamentalist sect.

The interesting thing in this case was not so much the process itself, or that a Catholic priest begins a loving relationship with one of the congregation members. It has happened many times. The interesting thing was - for me - to monitor the development that Martin went through. When he was a Catholic priest in the outskirts he was known at every opportunity in guiding the church in the right celibate lifestyle, but nevertheless, it was precisely this norm, which he himself was not able to follow. I remember a personal conversation that I had with him while he was still a Catholic priest and myself were the convert's students. It took place in his vicarage in the outskirts and here he enjoined me that adherence to the Catholic Church demanded acceptance of the church's moral standards. Where in the Bible these standards - exactly - was set, he could not explain, but he referred to the Catholic Catechism, which made it clear that sex belongs in marriage and contraception was banned. I did happen to know that Martin had a child with one of his mistresses from his communist period, so I could guess that his present conviction of the joy of celibacy was something he had acquired at a later date. But I was not entirely convinced of his exhortations. In the Catholic Church the many rumors, and I had heard some stories about Martin, who may not all were equally credible. But on the other hand, I also believe that there is rarely "smoke without fire." All this was confirmed to me when Martin moved in with one of his parishioners and resigned from the Catholic Church. What a surprise it must have been for his congregation.

* Kozon's new leadership

Another negative impression of the new management style during Czeslaw Kozon I got, when in year 2000 I started a website under the name Ansgar.dk. I had for several years been active on the internet, and it was natural for me to write about what I was interested in, and one of the things I was very interested in was the difference between the Lutheran and Catholic teaching. I knew quite a bit about the subject because I had examined it quite thoroughly with several of my convert's educators, and I had read several pamphlets, published before the Second Vatican Council, where the difference between Catholicism and Protestantism were reviewed. It must be said that I also knew that the Catholic Church in our time, not to the same extent as before, could recognize that difference.

A little history about this, I remember clearly. A few months after I had been accepted in the church, I visited the Catholic library in Stengade and asked if they had a book on the Reformation. I thought I should be able to find such a book, written from the Catholic point of view, in a Catholic library. Everything I had learned in school when I was a child was that the Reformation in 1536 had been a good thing, and that the church had previously been characterized by hypocrisy and indulgences.

I felt that could not be the whole truth, so I needed to read another angle to the story than the one I was introduced to in the Danish school. The surprise was therefore great when the librarian told me that "this kind of books we have not." I was told that I had to go to a public library if I would know more about the Reformation. But how could I benefit from the books in a public library, knowing that all these books were about the reformation seen from a protestant point of view? This was not possible, so I decided to make my own list of what separated the Catholic faith from Lutheranism. It was about human vision, free will, the church's global nature of the sacraments, priestly consecration and several other things.

I wish that I had had a similar list when I was a convert student, for it was certainly much easier to understand and grasp the Catholic religion, when you can see where it differs from other religions. I therefore made this list, which contained ten points, and this list I put on Ansgar.dk. And there came an immediate response. The Christian paper Kristeligt Dagblad make full-page article in which they sought to belittle my website, and Catholic Orientation spent a editorial leader for the same purpose. Neither of the two articles could detect any kind of errors in my texts, but they both believed that such listings would create unnecessary animosity between Catholics and Protestants.

I could certainly not agree, for all my family and all my friends were Protestants, and none of these had expressed that they were insulted, although they very well knew my views for many years. I also got a number of positive responses from other readers of the website, and everything indicated that I had written something substantial. It was therefore not entirely comprehensible to me, that bishop Kozon wrote a letter to the editor of Kristeligt Dagblad and told the readers of the paper that my list did not express the teaching of the Catholic Church. And he was wrong. If my listings of the differences between Catholic and Protestant faith was not real, then what was the purpose for me of converting to the latter? If Protestantism and Catholicism is the same, why should we encourage people to convert, as I had done?

* Moral considerations

In order not to make the present story too long, I will not tell you about the many *good* experiences I have had in the Catholic Church; the many beautiful fairs, the joy of praying to the Virgin Mary, the lovely song and music and a lot of nice people. I do not wonder clues that this church has thrived in 2.000 years, and that it is still able to attract new people, despite various scandals and a critical press. But what had once brought me to the church, was not its liturgical beauty or the nice people, but its faith and its humanity. I agreed with a view of humanity that is clearly distinct from the

Lutheran, and I certainly was not looking for something that was more or less the same.

Already half a year before I joined the church, I started to go regularly to Mass on Sundays. I did not quite understand what happened in this show, but I saw it as something beautiful, like a kind of play, which aimed to bring participants into closer connection to God. But the Catholic Church is more than fair. All Catholics receive without payment the Catholic magazine (Katolsk Orientering), and here we can follow various debates, and it certainly interested me. But there were still the same old things, that I did not agree with, that is the Church's position on contraception.

That sex is permitted only within marriage, I was aware of, but why the sexual act was only legitimate if it was intended to create new life, I was unable to see anything sensible in. The purpose of marriage exclusively would be to have children can be justified rationally, if you live in a society that is threatened by invasion and war, and whose survival is dependent on how many troops you can recruit. So it is reasonable that the church helps to increase the number of children by using its moral teachings.

But it is not such a society in which we live, so I cannot see the reasonableness of church teaching. Whether it can be justified by biblical texts, I do not care, because the Bible is a book written by humans. It is full of errors. If not a moral standard can be justified rationally, I cannot respect it, and the problem was not less, as the previously mentioned Torben Riis - a fanatical advocate of the idea that contraception is sin - was the editor of the Church magazine.

This meant that the right-wing tendency, which for several years had characterized the magazine, got even more widespread. Interest in the world's real problems gave way to continuous propaganda for the church's sexual teachings with the purpose of educating the Danish Catholics to the norms that Paul VI had set out in his encyclical Humanae Vitae.

Torben Riis did not argue rationally for his views, but stressed again and again as his best argument for the sinfulness of contraception that is was "in accordance with the teachings of the Church." He did not hide his warm support for US President George Bush, who opposed abortion. Therefore, there was also not a single critical word when the Americans bombed civilians in Iraq and Afghanistan and when the Israelis did the same in Gaza. "The end justifies the means" was probably the editor's position, and it was certainly in accordance with the former mayor and honorary member of the Danish liberal party, Erling Tidemann, from whom he had taken over the position as an editor from.

Riis had, as mentioned, ten children so no one could doubt that he and his wife followed the guidelines that Paul VI had formulated, but for some reason, one always kept the editor's voluminous crowd of children hidden in the portrait articles that the magazine wrote about him. Perhaps he was ashamed. Or, he could see that the church's moral logic was fragile. On the one hand we were told that they should not use contraceptives because it was God's will that you should have children when you had sex. But at the same time you had to like to use the so-called Billings method ("safe" periods), which - according to its advocates - would be just as effective as artificial contraception. There was a clear double standard here.

Why God had so much against the contraception pill, but allowed spouses to limit the number of children by using "safe" periods, one could not get answers to. A rationale was apparently not so when the topic was discussed, referring to the editor "church tradition" and it seemed very little convincing. If it was sinful to avoid children with birth control pills, so I suppose it was sinful too to avoid children using safe periods. The Catholic teaching - in Torben Riis's version - seemed to me to be untrustworthy, and I wondered how such a rightwing papist could be used as editor of the Catholic magazine. But it was bishop Kozon's decision.

I also found other problems with the Catholic teaching about marriage. The marriage understood as a sacrament given by the parties to each other, is creating uncertainty. Catholics cannot be divorced, but they can have declared their marriage invalid. This happens, for example if one of the parties had not entered into the marriage voluntarily or if one has had a mental reservation, when one gave marriage vow. The problem is that neither party has any opportunity to find out whether the other had a mental reservation when the marriage took place, and therefore it is impossible for Catholics to know certainly whether they are married or not. If the marriage was contracted under the ideal circumstances, then it is valid, but if one party has a history of mental reservation, then it is invalid. That you just cannot know before marriage is tried by a church's court of law, which the fewest marriages get done. Therefore Catholics do not know for sure whether they are married or not, that is, in the sacramental sense of the word. They can believe and hope for it, but they do not know.

Doubt was therefore starting to arise. In addition to the above considerations, I also found other points where I had to be critical, the Ten Commandments for example. Should we always abide by them? No, I mean when not. For me it is not true that one must never lie (the 8th bid), because there are situations where lying is the best way to solve a moral problem. Nor is it true that you cannot kill (the 5th bid), because there are situations where it is necessary. The suit does not mean that you always have to "turn the other cheek", because if you do, then it teaches people not to take it into account, and there are certain norms that people must be forced to respect. Overall, one can say that the Christian morality consists of a number of doctrines that can inspire, but they must never be loved.

It must always be the mind and the personal conscience, which will decide how to act in a given situation. But unfortunately I have difficulty seeing that that is what Kozon's editors are suggesting. They used their power to agitate for a right-wing and traditionalistic outlook, which I do not share. And unfortunately there is no alternative. In other countries with more Catholics, one can leave the parish and thus free themselves from a bishop who you do not like.

But you cannot in Denmark where the country is too small. In this country, the Catholic Church is actually not Catholic, it is a small sect.

* Judean surprises

When I joined the church, I did not know so much about the history that I know today. But I learned in my converts teaching about the last great ecumenical council (Second Vatican Council, 1962 - 65). I just did not have the great understanding of the connection between the war and the council, and no understanding at all of the comprehensive changes that the church had undergone after that council.

Today I want to question if the Catholic Church - after Vatican II - can be described as a Christian church, but I did not do that when I went to convert teaching. Doubt came with time, as I got more experience, which all pointed in the same direction. I began to doubt if the Church really believed in the words from the Creed and all the things I had learned in teaching to become a convert. I know today that this is not the case, but it took long before I found out about it, and it required hard work. Therefore, I have full understanding for the vast majority of Catholics who never come to the same realization. They have neither the time nor the strength to go through the same learning process that I went through, and maybe it also does not matter. They are satisfied about how things work now, and that makes them happy.

My first experience that was something that was hidden from me was when I attended a course at the converts Magleås in 1996. One of the teachers was a Vietnamese priest who had to give a presentation on the church's history. At one point he came to say that a certain ratio in the church was due to "Jewish influence". This expression puzzled me, and when we later on could ask questions, I asked what he had meant. I was sure that the priest knew very well what he had said as quoted, and several of the other participants had also noticed it. But nevertheless he claimed now that he could not remember having used this expression, and he did not want to comment on this issue any further. It was my distinct impression that the course leader had given him the advice, not to say more, and to play ignorant. And maybe it was good advice, because the alternative could have been a longer discussion.

What I speculated over was the fact that the priest had even dared to say such a thing. I had never heard anything like it, and there had to be something about it when a minister and speaker had said it, even if he pretended suddenly to have forgotten it again. What he had said could have been his own position, but he was well educated as a Catholic priest, and therefore spoke not only on their own behalf? At least I had - until then - never met people who openly admitted that the Jews had any influence in the Catholic Church. I could not help but wonder what it was that the priest had thought of? What influence did the Jews have? What was it that the priest no longer dared to talk about?

Next time I encountered the Jewish within the Catholic Church, was when I was at Mass in Lyngby, where the local parish priest Nibler appeared with a robe with a blue David star sewn on. It seemed to me strange that a Catholic priest advertised Judaism, since this show was a celebration of Jesus' Cross-offering that is a symbolic representation of the killing of Jesus made by the Jews had, and that was - in my opinion - the core of the Christian faith. But for Nibler Christianity was apparently not very different from Judaism, and - like others - he thought that you were able to be Catholic and Jew at once. The time when the Jews were called "God-killers" was over, and the fact that Jesus of the New Testament calls the synagogue "the synagogue of Satan" (Revelation. 13/9) was now forgotten in the Catholic Church. This surprised me and I started thinking about when this shift had happened.

I always went to Mass with Father Dorn at Sankt Augustin Church or at the Sacrament Church with Pater Sahner. Both places I met the Jewish thinking again and again and I now had gotten used to think of it as part of the Catholic belief. I did not think much about what had once been the difference between the two religions. I met several people who told me that they were Jews and Catholics at the same time or that they were Catholics who came from a Jewish family. And it was interesting. In order to follow the Jewish faith, one is Jew if one's mother is Jew, even if you are baptized or - formally - belong to another church. Such people are called "crypto-jews" and it occurred to me that there was a quite a few of those in the Catholic Church.

I also heard about the French Archbishop Lustiger, who many believed could be the new pope when John Paul II died. Also, he spoke openly that he was Jew and Catholic at one time. And it fit very well into what I learned in Sacrament Church, with the sympathetic pastor Sahner, who came from Germany. He always told about his trips to Israel, and about what he claimed was "the Jewish doctrine" about one thing or another. Always we were told that Judaism is based on the Torah (= Old Testament), and that Jews and Christians thus had a common basis for their beliefs, which may mean that the two religions were not opposed to each other, but that they almost were identical. It was therefore not very much surprised when Pastor Sahner warned the congregation against going in the cinema to see Mel Gibson's movie "Passion of Christ" (2004), which showed Jesus' judgment, torture, suffering and death from the Gospel narrative. This did pastor Sahner not like because thereby one is suggesting that the Jews were responsible for Jesus' death, and that kind one must be careful to say in Germany, where the pastor came from. In Germany you can go to jail for claiming things like that.

* Williamson affair

My final break with the Catholic Church came as a result of the so-called Williamson affair. Richard Williamson was the bishop of the traditionalist Pius X's company that Pope Benedict XVI had decided to integrate in the Catholic Church. The company was founded by the French Archbishop Lefebvre in 1970 as a protest against the liberal reforms by the Second Vatican Council. The company had, since its foundation, worked outside the Catholic Church, in the legal sense, while its leaders recognize the pope and the church's teaching, as it appeared in the Catholic tradition. Some of the decisions of the Second Vatican Council however they disagreed on, and therefore they had all been ex-communized. But it was not a big problem for the company as they had several legitimate consecrated bishops, as well as lots of young priests.

In March 2009, Pope Benedict XVI stated that he had lifted the excommunication of the schismatic company and that he would begin negotiating for its reopening as a legal entity in the Catholic Church. But that was not what caught the attention of the press. It did in return, when Swedish TV - a few days after the notification from the Vatican - could bring excerpts of an interview which they had made with one of its bishops, Richard Williamson. In this interview the bishop had expressed that he did not believe the story of the 6 million Jews, and that he did not believe that Hitler had executed prisoners in gas chambers. His view was well in line with the extensive revisionist literature, but the fact is that 99.9 % of the world population does not know this literature. Many know that it exists, but almost no one has read it. In several European countries, it is even forbidden to read such books, and to express such views, and when Bishop Williamson was in Germany when the interview was conducted, there was perhaps a basis for prosecution. The interview was recorded in autumn 2008 so much indicated that the Swedish television producer had deliberately waited to publish it for that special occasion. And it worked.

The story was spread throughout the world, and rarely have I seen a more obvious example of what the previously mentioned Vietnamese priest who had once been referring to as "Jewish influence". He had been right. It was clear that the forces that govern the international press, has little love for the Catholic Church, at least not in the form that it had before the Second Vatican Council, and that was what Richard Williamson was an exponent for.

I could only feel respect for this man who so courageously had given his opinion, knowing that it could cost him dearly. And it did. He was fired from his job as head of a seminary, and he was expelled from Argentina, where he had lived for many years. The Pope and a number of German cardinals and bishops got busy assuring the world and the Judean controlled press in the United States, that Catholics naturally "believe in the Holocaust." Already a week after Williamson's interview was published, the pope held a meeting at the Vatican with the Jewish leaders from the United States. Naturally, he could assure them that the cooperation and the sectarian community of Jews was one of the key points of Catholic doctrine. It put an ease on the Catholic bishops in Germany and elsewhere, and their demands for the Pope's departure was withdrawn.

During the heated debate the German pope repeatedly stated that the Catholic Church firmly believed in the Holocaust and the 6 million killed Jews. Several Catholic bishops and cardinals, as well as the Vatican's ambassador to Israel, said even that "one cannot be Catholic, if you do not believe in the Holocaust." The so-called Holocaust deniers therefore had to realize that they were not Catholics, even though many of these were actually born and raised in a Catholic environment (e.g. Robert Faurisson and Germar Rudolf).

And here we are at the end of the story, because although I quite agree with Richard Williamson. I have spent many years studying Hitlerism and related Holocaust history, and I am fully convinced that this - like so many other propagandistic descriptions from the war - is based on falsehood. I feel no urge to say something good about Nazism, but I prefer to criticize Hitler for what he did, such as that he killed 27 million Russians, rather than something that he did not. It's war victors who write history, but it is not the same as this victor is always right. So I agree with Bishop Williamson, but has otherwise difficult to see what his and my views on WW2 has to do with the Catholic faith. It says nothing about the Holocaust, in the Bible, in church documents, in the Creed, or the Catholic catechism. How can the official representatives of the Pope say that one cannot be Catholic, if you do not believe in the Holocaust? What do these two things to do with each other?

As mentioned earlier, I am aware that the Catholic Church, in the aftermath of the Second World War, has changed its teachings and philosophy. Now there is no real difference between Jews and Catholics, and the Zionist Jews and the story of the Holocaust is the fundamental "mystery" which is to be believed. For Zionism and racism in Israel, the story of the Holocaust is as important as the story of the crucifixion of Jesus is for Christians. Without this history, there was no Catholic Church.

But unlike Jews, so we Christians do not force the followers of other religions to believe in the Christian mythology. This we keep to ourselves, and we give other people the right to believe what they think is true. It is therefore difficult for me to understand why the Catholic Church must force everyone to believe in the Jewish mythology. What's the problem with Williamson and approximately 50 % of the world's population and of the Muslims do not believe in the gas chambers and 6 million? Winston Churchill did not write one word about gas chambers in his 5 volume history of the 2. Word War. Was he a holocaust-denier too?

Why must all people believe the same? Is the difficulty that the Jews do not even fully believe in this demonic history? Or is it that you want to ensure the story of the Holocaust, because that act as moral covers for war crimes by the US and Israel commits and the areas they have occupied? I do not know, but all experiences say that Jewish interest groups are working diligently to restrict freedom of expression in the countries where they have influence. They claim to be in favor of democracy, but the premise of democracy - freedom of speech - they do not like.

Bishop Kozon excelled not particularly in this debate. He was on TV a couple of times where he reaffirmed the Church's faith in the Holocaust and denounced Richard Williamson. I therefore wrote a small article and a letter to the editor of Catholic Orientation. Here, I pointed out that Pius XII - like Richard Williamson - not even thought of what today is called the Holocaust. Although he repeatedly protested against Nazism, then he never mentioned anything about the deliberate mass extermination, gas chambers or 6 million killed Jews that one must assume that he would have known if it was actually true.

Poland is a Catholic country, and the commander and many of the guards at Auschwitz were Catholics. I also pointed out that the Jewish Rabbi Benjamin Blech in 2001 published a book entitled "*The secret of the Hebrew words*" and where he showed that the number "6 million" comes from the Hebrew original text of the third book of Genesis (ch. 25;10), and thus cannot be anything but a myth. But neither of the two texts Catholic Orientation wanted to publish. They preferred the Jewish sacred mythology that now apparently was binding faith for Catholics. And it is related to the fact that several Catholic bishops in the past 30 years has made known that they did not believe that the story of Jesus was historically accurate.

Take for example the Catholic "Dutch Catechism", which claims that the virgin birth is a myth. This kind of thinking is called for "narrative theology" and you can read in the papal Bible commission writings that it is fully permissible to have such views in the Catholic Church. However this freedom of thought does not apply with regards to the Holocaust. Here one must not talk about myths, because here it is sacred to the Jews. It is part of the Western world's moral self-understanding. The Catholic Church's teaching authority thinks more about their relation to the killers of Christ than they think about the Gospel, therefore one can wonder whether the church can still be called Christian.

Although I believe that the answer is "no" if the word is understood in its original meaning. Catholics are not Christians, and the same can be said of the evangelical Zionists in the US, which has such a great influence on US foreign policy. The feeling that I got shortly after my membership in the church, appeared then to be true. There was something that was kept hidden for me, something I had to know. I am therefore pleased about my mental reservation, because when the church hides its teachings for me and other Christians, we also have the right to hide our faith for the church. When you do not have the right to say what you think, then you have to lie, and that is what the church is forcing its members to do.

Formally, I have not left the church, but I am no more going to Mass and do not participate in church activities. I think that the church is stupefied and that its leader is unworthy. Pope Benedikt XVI (the old nazi) failed to visit the Christians in the occupied Gaza when he visited Israel in spring 2009, but he had plenty of time to visit the Israeli Holocaust museum Yad Vashem.

It shows what the Pope believes and what he does not care about. And the museum he visited does not hide the fact, that enemies of the Jews - both in the past and in the present - are the Christians. Commandant of Auschwitz (Rudolf Höess) during Hitler, was a Catholic, and no teaching authority threatened him with either excommunication or other sanctions. If the Holocaust in the Jewish interpretation is true, then the Catholic Church in the highest degree co-responsible, and to such an extent that there is good sense in Elie Wiesel's words, that what died in Auschwitz was not the Jews but the Christian religion.

You have a problem in the Catholic Church, and the way you are trying to solve it, is untrustworthy. Although I do not want to spend time and invest money in this organization, which I perceive as embarrassing. I converted to the Catholic faith, because I could join the Catholic view of human nature and the Catholic morality. Because I am anti-racist, do not believe in a God who nurtures his chosen people at the expense of others. But I also realized that it - unfortunately is not this doctrine, which the Catholic Church professes after the Second Vatican Council. I am in favor of this Council's teaching that all may go to heaven (including Muslims), and I like the modern liturgy. But apart from that, I have a hard time finding something good to say about the church today. It works as an appendage to another religion, and thus an utterly superfluous.

Nothing lasts forever, but the reigning pope from Germany (Benedikt XVI), we should not wait for any change coming from him. The prospects for restoring the church as a Christian organization, is long. Maybe it will never happen, and we only need to note that even one of the modern world players have had to surrender to the forces which already controls the media and political life in the Western world. Where the church once was the center of the confrontation with Judaism, then it is today the center of criticism of Islam. The decay of the church is expressed in plain apostasy from the Christian faith, which includes the fact that the number of abortions in the world's most Catholic country - Italy - is among the highest in the world.

A series of pedophilia scandals among Catholic priests have also shown that the church is not even able to convince its own employees about the Christian ideals. And it's probably not surprising, because who can believe in a church that does not even dare to discuss its own story. In Germany and several other European countries, it is forbidden to question the Holocaust, and the church does not protest. Pius XII would have been put in prison, had he lived in one of these countries today. But nevertheless Catholics seek to make him a saint. Double standards know no boundaries. Richard Williamson must not serve as bishop of this church because he did not believe the story about the gas chambers, but Benedict XVI is allowed to be pope, although he has been a member of the Hitler Jugend and soldier under Hitler. So it is worse to doubt the Holocaust, than it is to be partly responsible for its execution!

The logic is hard to follow, but as with so much else, it certainly tells Catholics that it is a "mystery". And here the aforementioned Elie Wiesel, today's best-known Holocaust prophet, probably provides them right. He said at one point that there were historical events, *"which had not happened, but nevertheless was true. And other events that had happened, yet not true"*. For Catholics Holocaust is probably one of these events. But for me it is otherwise. The only mystery I can spot is how people who call themselves

Christians, may betray the crucified Jesus in the way the German Pope and his followers are doing. The only consolation I have is the one you find in the old wisdom that *"you can always fool some people and all the people from time to time. But you cannot always fool all the people."* I hope that this also applies in the Catholic Church.